T.S

T.S. AVINI

ETF Investing Simplified

Build a Safe, Long-Term Portfolio Without Complexity

by T.S. AVINI

Table of Contents

1. Introduction to ETF Investing: Understanding the Basics
2. The Evolution of Exchange-Traded Funds: A Brief History
3. Why ETFs? Exploring the Benefits Over Traditional Investing
4. Types of ETFs: Equity, Bond, Commodity, and Beyond
5. Understanding Risk and Return in ETF Investments
6. Building Blocks of a Strong ETF Portfolio: Diversification Strategies
7. How to Choose the Right ETFs: Criteria and Tools for Assessment
8. The Role of Indexes in ETF Investing: A Closer Look
9. Analyzing ETF Performance: Key Metrics and Indicators
10. Tax Efficiency and ETFs: Maximizing After-Tax Returns
11. Low-Cost Investing: Understanding ETF Fees and Expenses
12. Long-Term Investment Strategies with ETFs: Setting Goals and Taking Action
13. Managing Market Volatility: Protecting Your ETF Portfolio
14. The Psychology of Investing: Overcoming Emotional Decisions
15. Common Mistakes in ETF Investing and How to Avoid Them
16. Navigating Financial Crises: ETFs During Market Turbulence
17. Sustainable and Ethical Investing: ESG and Themed ETFs
18. Technological Tools for ETF Investors: From Research to Execution
19. Future Trends in ETF Investing: What to Watch For
20. Conclusion: Simplifying the Path to Financial Independence with ETFs

Chapter 1: Introduction to ETF Investing: Understanding the Basics

In the bustling world of finance, abundance reigns—not just in the form of wealth or assets but in the sheer variety of investment options available to individuals looking to grow their capital. From stocks and bonds to mutual funds and more exotic derivatives, choosing the right investment vehicle can feel like a daunting task.

Of late, however, a simpler and increasingly popular choice has emerged—Exchange Traded Funds, or ETFs. This chapter unravels the fundamental aspects of ETF investing, presenting it as an accessible yet potent option for budding and seasoned investors alike.

What are ETFs?

I've seen this happen before: At their core, ETFs are investment funds that are traded on stock exchanges, much like individual stocks.

An ETF holds assets such as stocks, commodities, or bonds, and generally operates with an arbitrage mechanism designed to keep trading close to its net asset value, though deviations can occasionally occur. ETFs offer the flexibility of a stock and the diversification benefits of a mutual fund.

When you invest in an ETF, you purchase shares that represent a fraction of a portfolio designed to track a specific index.

Popular indices such as the S&P 500, the NASDAQ, or international commodities indexes are often mirrored by ETFs, granting investors exposure to a broad array of assets in a single transaction. This characteristic makes ETFs a convenient tool for investors who aim for diversification without the burden of managing multiple trades or posessing considerable capital.

A Brief History of ETFs

Let's not forget, The origin of ETFs can be traced back to the early 1990s. The very first ETF, known as SPDR (pronounced 'spider'), was introduced by State Street Global Advisors in 1993.

It was designed to track the S&P 500 index and served as a prototype for future ETF structures. The concept quickly gained traction due to its cost-effectiveness and simplicity, triggering a proliferation of ETFs over the following decades. Today, thousands of ETFs exist, each catering to different investment preferences and strategies, from broad market indices to niche sectors and thematic investing.

How Do ETFs Work?

The success of ETFs lies in their structural simplicity and efficiency. On a basic operational level, ETFs are created and managed through a process called "creation and redemption.

" This involves authorized participants (large institutional investors) exchanging securities (stocks, bonds, etc.) for ETF shares. These authorized participants ensure that supply and demand for ETF shares remain balanced, which typically helps maintain the ETF's price in line with its underlying assets.

Interestingly enough, Investors can buy and sell shares of an ETF throughout the trading day, offering a level of liquidity and flexibility akin to that of stocks.

This intraday trading capability distinguishes ETFs from mutual funds, which are priced at the end of the trading day. The ease with which ETFs can be exchanged makes them an attractive option for both long-term investors and day traders.

Advantages of ETF Investing

Diversification

Believe it or not, ETFs provide instant diversification, one of the most significant benefits for investors.

By purchasing a single ETF, investors gain exposure to a basket of securities that could include hundreds or even thousands of individual assets. This diversification reduces the risk associated with holding individual securities, such as stocks or bonds, where significant events affecting a single entity can have adverse impacts on the investment.

Cost-Effectiveness

ETFs are usually passively managed, meaning they track specific indices rather than rely on active fund managers to select securities.

This passive management style often results in lower expense ratios compared to mutual funds. Additionally, because ETFs are traded like stocks, investors typically pay lower transaction fees compared to traditional mutual funds.

Flexibility and Liquidity

The ability to trade ETFs throughout the day provides investors with the flexibility to respond promptly to market conditions, a feature not available with mutual funds.

The substantial liquidity of most ETFs ensures investors can enter and exit positions with minimal price distortion, though this can vary based on the ETF's underlying assets.

Transparency

In real life, ETFs typically disclose their holdings publicly on a daily basis.

This transparency allows investors to see exactly what assets their money is exposed to, providing clarity that many mutual funds, which disclose holdings less frequently, do not.

Risks Associated with ETFs

While ETFs are associated with various benefits, they are not without risks. The following are essential considerations investors should heed:

Market Risk

Just like any other investment, ETFs are subject to market risks.

The value of an ETF can fluctuate with the broader market or the specific index it tracks. Economic environments, geopolitical tensions, and investor sentiment can all lead to fluctuations in ETF value.

Tracking Error

At first glance, Tracking error arises when an ETF's performance deviates from that of its target index.

While typically minimal, tracking errors can occur due to factors such as management fees, cash holdings, and the timing of dividend distributions within the ETF.

Complexity of Inverse and Leveraged ETFs

Some ETFs aim to achieve multiples of the inverse performance of their target index.

These leveraged and inverse ETFs can be more complex and risky than traditional ETF products, and they generally involve higher fees. They are primarily designed for short-term trading strategies rather than long-term investment and may not perform as expected over longer periods.

In real life, ## The Role of ETFs in a Long-Term Investment Strategy

ETFs can serve as a robust foundation for building a long-term investment portfolio.

By selecting a diversified range of ETFs that align with specific financial goals and risk tolerance, investors can construct a balanced portfolio tailored to their individual needs. Whether you are aiming for capital growth, fixed income, or a specific sector focus, there is likely an ETF suited to your objectives.

Choosing low-cost, broad market ETFs is a prudent strategy for investors who want to mirror market growth while minimizing costs.

Meanwhile, sector-specific or thematic ETFs might appeal to those willing to embrace higher risk for the potential of higher returns. Ultimately, the versatility and accessibility of ETFs make them a compelling choice for investors at all experience levels.

As strange as it sounds, In conclusion, ETFs present a streamlined, accessible, and cost-effective way to engage in the world of investing.

By understanding the fundamental mechanics, advantages, and potential risks of ETFs, investors are better equipped to make informed decisions about how these versatile instruments fit into their long-term objectives. As you continue through this book, you'll gain deeper insights into building a safe, efficient, and effective ETF-based portfolio tailored to your financial journey.

Chapter 2: The Evolution of Exchange-Traded Funds: A Brief History

The financial world is often likened to a complex ecosystem where instruments and products evolve, adapt, and sometimes fade away over time.

Among the most remarkable products to emerge in recent decades is the Exchange-Traded Fund (ETF). Understanding ETFs' journey from inception to their current popularity offers investors valuable insight into their role and potential in a diversified portfolio.

To fully appreciate the significance of ETFs in the modern investment landscape, it is crucial to begin with their roots. The genesis of ETFs can be traced back to the early 1980s, a time when the investment community was seeking new ways to access broad market indexes.

In 1981, the Toronto Stock Exchange launched an instrument known as the Toronto Index Participation Shares (TIPS), which allowed investors to buy into the TSE 35 and TSE 100 indices. Though promising, TIPS were short-lived due to regulatory challenges. Nevertheless, they laid the groundwork for future developments.

It's worth noting that The concept of a pooled investment vehicle that trades like a stock but offers the diversification of a mutual fund was seen as revolutionary. The breakthrough came in January 1993 when the American Stock Exchange introduced the Standard & Poor's Depositary Receipts, commonly known as SPDRs or "Spiders.

" These were the first successful exchange-traded products available in the United States, designed to track the S&P 500 Index. Their instantaneous success marked the birth of modern ETFs as we know them today.

SPDRs captivated investors with their unique advantages. Unlike mutual funds, they could be traded on an exchange throughout the trading day, offering liquidity and flexibility.

They also generally boasted lower expense ratios compared to traditional mutual funds due to their passive management style, which tracks indices rather than actively selecting securities. These attributes addressed key investor concerns regarding flexibility, cost-efficiency, and diversification.

Throughout the late 1990s and early 2000s, the ETF market began to diversify rapidly.

Fund managers introduced ETFs that tracked a wide variety of benchmarks, including international indices, sector-specific baskets, and later, commodities like gold and oil. The allure of ETFs extended across different investor profiles—from retail investors and day traders to institutional money managers—each finding unique advantages in these versatile tools.

Many people don't realize this, but The financial crisis of 2008-2009 acted as a crucible, testing the resilience and integrity of financial instruments worldwide.

During this tumultuous time, many investors turned to the transparency and low cost of ETFs as an alternative to actively managed funds, which suffered from higher fees and unpredictable performance. The crisis accelerated the shift towards passive investing, as investors increasingly sought out index-tracking ETFs to weather market volatility and storm financial uncertainties.

Technological advancements also played a significant role in ETF evolution.

The rise of online trading platforms made it easier than ever for individuals to buy and sell ETFs directly, democratizing access and empowering a new generation of investors. These platforms reduced barriers to entry and increased the frequency and volume of trades, allowing ETFs to flourish in a tech-driven landscape that prioritizes rapid execution and real-time information.

As the 2010s progressed, the ETF market continued to innovate.

The introduction of Smart Beta ETFs marked a further evolution, blending active and passive strategies by weighting stocks according to factors like volatility, dividend yield, or other quantitative criteria rather than simply market capitalization. These ETFs aim to provide better risk-adjusted returns, challenging the traditional differentiation between active and passive investing.

Believe it or not, Moreover, the emergence of thematic ETFs appealed to those seeking to align investments with specific growth trends, such as clean energy, robotics, or artificial intelligence.

This new wave of ETFs broadened the appeal of exchange-traded products, offering a tailored approach to investors keen on capitalizing on specific economic narratives and technological advancements.

Another significant development in recent years is the rise of Environmental, Social, and Governance (ESG) ETFs.

As awareness and interest in sustainable investing have grown, so too has the demand for funds that align with investors' values. ESG ETFs represent a fusion of ethical considerations and financial performance, catering to those who wish to ensure their investments reflect a commitment to positive environmental and social impact.

Regulatory changes have also impacted ETF evolution, with authorities around the world recognizing their value and establishing frameworks to govern their issuance and trading.

In the United States, for example, the Securities and Exchange Commission (SEC) approved a new rule in 2019 that allowed ETF issuers greater flexibility in creating funds, further accelerating innovation and expansion in the sector.

The ETF landscape today is vibrant and multifaceted, offering a vast array of options to suit almost any investment strategy or preference.

From nascent beginnings to becoming an integral part of the financial toolkit, ETFs have reshaped the way investors approach the market, combining the best attributes of stocks and mutual funds into one attractive package.

In conclusion, the evolution of ETFs reflects broader trends in finance: the shift towards cost-efficiency, transparency, and access. By understanding their history, investors can better appreciate the strategic role ETFs play in building a balanced, long-term portfolio.

As ETFs continue to evolve, they promise to meet the ever-changing needs of both individual and institutional investors, offering a simplified yet powerful means to engage with the financial markets. In the subsequent chapters, we will explore how to harness the full potential of ETFs to build a resilient and diversified investment portfolio, free from unnecessary complexity but rich in opportunity.

Chapter 3: Why ETFs? Exploring the Benefits Over Traditional Investing

In the ever-evolving world of investing, Exchange-Traded Funds (ETFs) have emerged as a popular and accessible option for many investors.

But why have these financial instruments gained such traction, and how do they compare to traditional investing methods like individual stocks and mutual funds? This chapter delves into the key benefits of ETFs, providing a practical understanding of why they might be the right fit for your portfolio.

Accessibility and Simplicity

At first glance, One of the primary advantages of ETFs is their accessibility. Unlike other investment vehicles, ETFs can be bought and sold on stock exchanges, much like individual stocks.

This means that investors can enter and exit ETF positions with relative ease during market trading hours, which stands in stark contrast to mutual funds, which only trade at their net asset value at the end of the trading day. This liquidity provides traders more control over the timing of their transactions, potentially allowing them to capitalize on short-term market movements.

The simplicity of ETFs is another factor contributing to their popularity. With a single purchase, investors can gain exposure to a broad spectrum of assets, thereby achieving instant diversification.

This feature minimizes the need to engage in laborious stock picking, which requires significant research and expertise. ETFs typically track an index, such as the S&P 500 or the MSCI World Index, which already encompasses a diversified range of assets. For novice investors, this built-in diversification is particularly appealing as it helps spread risk without the requirement of managing multiple individual investments.

Cost Efficiency

Interestingly enough, Cost is a pivotal consideration in any investment strategy. ETFs generally come with lower expense ratios compared to mutual funds.

This is largely due to their passive management style, which seeks to replicate the performance of an index rather than outperform it through active management. Hence, there is less necessity for high-priced fund managers, resulting in lower management fees.

Beyond lower expense ratios, ETFs also tend to have fewer associated costs in terms of tax efficiency.

Because many ETFs employ an "in-kind" creation and redemption process, they can often avoid the capital gains distributions that burden mutual fund investors. This tax efficiency means that investors can potentially keep more of their returns over the long term, making ETFs a smart choice for those mindful of after-tax returns.

Transparency and Choice

In real life, Transparency is a significant edge that ETFs hold over traditional mutual funds.

Investors can see exactly what they own down to the last share, as most ETFs disclose their holdings daily. This level of transparency allows for better-informed decision-making and ensures that investors understand their exposure to different market risks.

The range of ETFs available on the market today caters to virtually any investment strategy. ETFs offer access to various asset classes, sectors, and geographic regions. Whether you wish to invest in U.

S. equities, emerging markets, commodities, or even specific themes like clean energy or technology, there's an ETF tailored to your interests. This multitude of options allows you to fine-tune your portfolio according to your risk tolerance and investment goals.

Flexible Strategies

It's worth noting that ETFs provide investors with a toolkit that can be adapted to various strategic approaches. Because they cover a broad range of asset classes, they can be used as building blocks for both conventional and innovative portfolio strategies.

Want to pursue a growth-oriented strategy? Consider allocating more to sector-specific or small-cap ETFs. Prefer a defensive stance? Fixed-income or dividend-focused ETFs might be more suitable.

Moreover, certain ETFs allow investors to employ advanced strategies like hedging or tactical asset allocation. For instance, leveraged ETFs can amplify returns on a short-term basis, while inverse ETFs could be used to profit from declining markets.

However, it's crucial to note that these specialized ETFs come with higher risks and may not be suitable for all investors. As always, understanding the product is key to ensuring it aligns with your investment goals.

Lower Barrier to Entry

Believe it or not, Compared to buying a diversified portfolio of individual stocks or mutual funds, which might require a significant initial investment, ETFs often have a lower barrier to entry.

Many ETFs do not have minimum investment requirements, making them accessible to investors with varying budget sizes. Fractional share investing, increasingly available at many brokerage firms, further reduces the barriers, allowing investors to buy a portion of an ETF share in alignment with the amount they wish to invest, rather than being restricted to whole shares.

This flexibility makes ETFs an enticing option for young or small-scale investors who are just starting to build their investment portfolios.

It democratizes the investment landscape, allowing more individuals to participate in market growth without requiring substantial capital.

The Future of Investing

In real life, As technology continues to advance and the financial landscape evolves, the popularity and variety of ETFs are set to grow.

They represent a melding of simplicity, cost efficiency, and choice, matched with the flexibility to adapt to numerous investment strategies. For many investors, the question isn't whether to include ETFs in their portfolio, but rather how to best utilize them to achieve their financial objectives.

Despite their many benefits, it's crucial for investors to do their due diligence.

Not all ETFs are created equal, and understanding the underlying assets, fees, and potential risks is important for maximizing your investment success. Each investor's financial situation and goals are unique, and while ETFs offer a variety of advantages, they must form part of a well-thought-out investment strategy that aligns with your individual goals.

In conclusion, ETFs stand out as a compelling alternative to traditional investing methods.

Their blend of accessibility, cost-efficiency, transparency, and strategic flexibility makes them a powerful tool in the investor's arsenal. Whether you're building your first portfolio or restructuring an existing one, understanding the benefits of ETFs can unlock a world of opportunities and position you for long-term success.

Chapter 4: Types of ETFs: Equity, Bond, Commodity, and Beyond

Exchange-traded funds, or ETFs, have fundamentally transformed the investment landscape, offering a blend of flexibility, diversity, and accessibility that appeals to both novice and seasoned investors.

Understanding the different types of ETFs is essential for building a robust, long-term portfolio. This chapter will delve into the primary categories of ETFs—equity, bond, and commodity—and explore other intriguing varieties that have emerged over time.

Equity ETFs: The Stock Market Simplified

As strange as it sounds, Equity ETFs are perhaps the most well-known among investors.

These ETFs provide exposure to a wide range of stocks, representing various sectors, industries, and geographies. The appeal of equity ETFs lies in their ability to offer instant diversification across multiple assets, with a single investment.

**1.

Broad Market ETFs:** These funds track well-known market indices like the S&P 500 or the Nasdaq-100, offering a slice of the entire stock market or specific segments. Investing in broad market ETFs is similar to capturing the overall performance of the market, making them a popular choice for long-term and passive investors.

**2.

Sector and Industry ETFs:** For those who wish to target specific parts of the economy, sector ETFs can be an attractive option. Whether you have a bullish outlook on technology, healthcare, or consumer goods, sector ETFs allow investors to concentrate their investments in specific economic areas while still enjoying diversification within that sector.

In real life, **3. International and Emerging Market ETFs:** Global diversification is crucial for any portfolio.

International ETFs give exposure to markets outside of the investor's home country. Emerging market ETFs delve even deeper, focusing on developing economies like Brazil, India, and China, offering potentially higher growth—but also increased risk.

**4.

Dividend ETFs:** For investors seeking income, dividend ETFs focus on stocks that regularly pay dividends. This generates a steady income stream, making them a suitable choice for retirees or anyone looking to reinforce an income-generating portfolio.

Bond ETFs: Fixed Income Made Easy

Interestingly enough, Bond ETFs are an excellent way for investors to gain exposure to the bond market, offering a more liquid and flexible approach than direct bond ownership.

They serve as a stabilizing force in a portfolio, counterbalancing the volatility of equities with steady, reliable returns.

1. Government Bond ETFs: These funds invest in bonds issued by governments, such as U.

S. Treasury bonds. Considered low-risk, they are ideal for risk-averse investors seeking safety and capital preservation.

**2.

Corporate Bond ETFs:** These involve bonds issued by companies, ranging from top-tier blue-chips to riskier high-yield or 'junk' bonds. Corporate bond ETFs are suitable for those seeking higher yields than government bonds typically provide, though this comes with increased risk.

Believe it or not, **3.

Municipal Bond ETFs:** Also known as muni bonds, these are issued by states and municipalities. They often provide tax-exempt income, making them appealing for investors in high tax brackets.

**4.

International and Emerging Market Bond ETFs:** For those looking to diversify beyond domestic fixed income, international bond ETFs, including those in emerging markets, offer exposure to global interest rate environments and foreign economic conditions.

Commodity ETFs: A Taste of Tangibility

Believe it or not, Commodity ETFs offer exposure to physical goods like gold, oil, or agricultural products.

Unlike direct investment in physical commodities, these ETFs are convenient and eliminate the need for physical storage.

**1.

Precious Metals ETFs:** Gold and silver ETFs are the most popular, viewed as a hedge against inflation and economic uncertainty. These ETFs track the price of underlying metals, allowing investors to speculate on price movements or use them as a store of value.

**2.

Energy Commodity ETFs:** These focus on oil, natural gas, or coal. Energy

ETFs are inherently linked to the fluctuations in global energy prices, making them volatile but sometimes rewarding investments.

**3.

Agriculture Commodity ETFs:** For investors who wish to tap into the food supply chain, agriculture ETFs cover commodities like wheat, corn, and soybeans. They can be highly speculative, influenced by weather conditions and global demand-supply dynamics.

Beyond Traditional: Innovative and Thematic ETFs

Investors have ever-evolving needs and interests, leading to the creation of unique ETFs that cater to niche markets or ideas.

Many people don't realize this, but **1.

Real Estate ETFs:** These funds invest in real estate investment trusts (REITs), offering exposure to the property market. They typically provide potential income through dividends and serve as a hedge against inflation.

**2.

Smart Beta ETFs:** These are designed to offer exposure to factors historically linked to outperforming market indices, such as value, size, momentum, and volatility. Smart beta ETF portfolios are managed according to precise rules, targeting those factors.

**3.

Thematic ETFs:** These funds focus on emerging trends or themes, such as clean energy, technological innovation, or demographic shifts. Thematic ETFs allow investors to align their investments with their worldview or interest areas, capturing growth opportunities in evolving industries.

Believe it or not, **4. Leveraged and Inverse ETFs:** For experienced investors with a strong risk tolerance, leveraged ETFs aim to amplify returns by using financial derivatives.

Conversely, inverse ETFs move opposite to the underlying index, representing bets against market performance. While these are sophisticated tools, they come with high risk and are generally not suited for long-term investment strategies.

Conclusion: Choosing the Right ETF for Your Portfolio

As you navigate the world of ETFs, the choices might seem overwhelming; however, understanding the purpose and characteristics of different ETF types can simplify the process. For a balanced portfolio, consider combining equity and bond ETFs to achieve growth and stability.

Complement these with commodity ETFs for diversification and thematic ETFs for exposure to future trends. Each ETF type serves a distinct role, and by aligning your investments with your financial goals, risk tolerance, and investment timeline, you can build a resilient, long-term portfolio without the hassle of managing individual securities.

In real life, In sum, ETFs provide an efficient, practical way to participate in the global investment ecosystem.

Whether your goal is capital appreciation, income generation, or risk mitigation, understanding these investment vehicles can unlock new opportunities on your financial journey.

Chapter 5: Understanding Risk and Return in ETF Investments

Investing is inherently about balancing risk and return, a concept that is especially critical when it comes to Exchange Traded Funds (ETFs).

These financial instruments offer a convenient and diversified way to engage in the stock market, but understanding the nuances of risk and return will bolster your confidence and competence as an investor. In this chapter, we'll demystify the interplay between risk and return in ETF investments, providing you with practical insights to help you make informed decisions.

Risk: Recognizing the Spectrum

In real life, At its core, risk in investing refers to the possibility that the actual returns from an investment will be lower than expected.

All investments carry some degree of risk, but the type and level of risk can vary significantly across different asset classes and even among different ETFs.

1.

Market Risk: Also known as systematic risk, market risk involves the potential for an entire market to decline in value, due to broad factors like economic downturns, political instability, or changes in monetary policy. ETFs, by nature of their diversification, tend to mitigate this risk somewhat compared to individual stocks, but they cannot eliminate it entirely.

2.

Credit Risk: For bond ETFs, this is a consideration that involves the risk of the bond issuer defaulting on its obligations. Government bond ETFs usually have less credit risk than corporate bond ETFs, but with potentially lower returns as a trade-off.

In real life, 3.

Liquidity Risk: This refers to the risk associated with not being able to buy or sell an investment without causing a significant impact on its price. ETFs are generally quite liquid, but not all ETFs are created equal; those that invest in niche markets or low-volume securities may carry higher liquidity risks.

4.

Tracking Error: This is specific to ETFs and refers to the risk that an ETF does not perfectly replicate the performance of its underlying asset or index. Some deviation is expected, but a consistently large tracking error could be a red flag.

Return: Setting Realistic Expectations

Many people don't realize this, but Return on investment (ROI) is the gain or loss generated on an investment relative to the amount of money invested.

The objective for any investor is to maximize returns while accepting a level of risk that is comfortable. Here's how you can navigate the landscape of returns in ETF investing:.

1.

Historical Performance: Examining past performance can provide insights, but it's crucial to remember the investment adage that "past performance is not indicative of future results. " Instead, look for consistent, long-term performance rather than short-term gains.

2.

Dividend Yields: Some ETFs, especially those invested in dividend-paying stocks, offer periodic income through dividends. High dividend yields can make an ETF attractive, but they might also indicate higher risk or lower capital appreciation potential.

I've seen this happen before: 3.

Total Return: This takes both capital gains and income into account, providing a comprehensive view of what you can expect from an ETF. It's important to evaluate this figure in the context of the ETF's risk profile.

4.

Expense Ratios: The cost of owning an ETF can have a substantial impact on net returns. Low-cost ETFs generally provide better net returns, given the same level of gross returns, due to the compounding effect of costs over time.

Risk-Return Trade-off: Balancing Act

The ultimate quest in investing is to find a suitable balance between risk and return.

This involves aligning your investment strategy with your financial goals, time horizon, and risk tolerance. Here's a practical approach to achieving this balance:.

1. **Risk Profiling:** Assessing your risk tolerance is crucial.

This involves understanding how much risk you are willing to take and how much temporary financial loss you can tolerate. Investors with high-risk tolerance might allocate more to equity-focused ETFs, while conservative investors might prefer bond or mixed-asset ETFs.

2.

Asset Allocation: Diversification across various asset types and sectors helps in spreading risk. ETFs are inherently diversified, but building a diversified portfolio of ETFs further mitigates unsystematic risk.

In real life, 3.

Periodic Review and Rebalancing: Market conditions and personal circumstances change over time, which necessitates regular review and adjustment of your portfolio. Rebalancing ensures that your portfolio remains aligned with your risk-return profile.

4.

Understanding Correlations: Different asset classes often behave differently under the same market conditions, such as stocks and bonds moving inversely. Utilize ETFs to capitalize on such correlations to enhance portfolio stability.

Practical Considerations and Strategies

Many people don't realize this, but 1.

Core-Satellite Strategy: Use broad market or index ETFs as the core of your portfolio for stable returns, and complement with smaller satellite ETFs in specific sectors or emerging markets to capture higher returns.

2.

Risk Mitigation Techniques: Consider incorporating ETFs that focus on defensive sectors like healthcare or consumer staples, or those that use strategies like low volatility to dampen portfolio risk during market downturns.

3.

Leveraged and Inverse ETFs: While these can offer high returns, they also come with increased risk and complexity. They are generally not recommended for long-term investors due to their compounding effects, which can lead to significant losses.

In real life, 4.

Educate and Adapt: Stay informed about market trends, economic indicators, and regulatory changes that impact the ETF landscape. Continuously educate yourself and adapt strategies as necessary.

Understanding the intricate relationship between risk and return in ETF investments is essential to crafting a resilient investment strategy.

Embrace the diversity and flexibility that ETFs offer, and use the insights in this chapter to navigate the ebbs and flows of the market with competence and confidence. As you develop your investment acumen, you'll be better equipped to achieve your financial goals with less complexity and more clarity.

Chapter 6: Building Blocks of a Strong ETF Portfolio: Diversification Strategies

In the realm of investment, diversification is often hailed as the only free lunch. This adage highlights the fundamental principle of not putting all your eggs in one basket.

The modern financial world offers many avenues to practice this principle effectively, and Exchange-Traded Funds (ETFs) are undeniably one of the most convenient vehicles for achieving diversification. In this chapter, we will delve into various strategies to diversify your ETF portfolio, ensuring you build a resilient and robust investment framework that can weather the storms of market fluctuations.

Understanding Diversification

To be honest, Diversification is the process of spreading your investments across various financial instruments, industries, and other categories to minimize risks.

The primary objective is risk management, reducing the exposure to any single asset or risk. Although diversification cannot eliminate all risks, it plays a crucial role in reducing unsystematic risks - those specific to a company or industry.

ETFs inherently offer diversification because each ETF contains a basket of securities.

However, creating a genuinely diversified portfolio requires thoughtful consideration of the types of ETFs you include, the asset classes they cover, and the proportion of each in your portfolio.

Core-Satellite Approach

Many people don't realize this, but A practical strategy for diversification is the core-satellite approach. This method involves splitting your portfolio into two segments: core investments and satellite investments.

The core is the foundation, typically consisting of broad-based, low-cost ETFs that represent the overall market or large segments of it. These might include total market ETFs or S&P 500 ETFs, offering stability and steady growth.

The satellite portion allows for tactical investments in more specific or niche areas where you might want to capitalize on particular opportunities or trends.

This might include sector-specific ETFs, international ETFs, or thematic ETFs that align with emerging market trends or technologies.

Geographical Diversification

Interestingly enough, Another layer of diversification is geographical. By investing globally, you spread risks associated with economic downturns or geopolitical tensions in any single region.

Consider blending domestic ETFs with international ones, ensuring exposure to both developed markets like Europe and Japan and emerging markets like Asia and Latin America. This mix can offer a balance of stability and growth potential, as different regions perform better at different times, partly due to varied economic conditions.

Sector Diversification

Sector diversification involves spreading investments across different industries or market sectors, such as technology, healthcare, finance, consumer goods, and energy.

This approach ensures that your portfolio isn't overly reliant on the performance of one sector, which can be particularly useful during market rotations when certain sectors fall out of favor while others gain traction.

When selecting sector ETFs, evaluate current economic conditions, trends, and valuations.

For example, during an economic recovery, cyclical sectors like consumer discretionary and industrials often perform well, while defensive sectors such as utilities and healthcare are usually more resilient during downturns.

Fixed Income and Equity Mix

While ETFs are predominantly known for equities, they are a superb tool for attaining diversification in fixed income as well.

A healthy portfolio blends both stocks and bonds, each providing different functions. Equities offer growth potential, albeit with higher volatility, while bonds typically provide income and reduced volatility.

The proportion of equity to fixed income should match your risk tolerance, investment goals, and time horizon.

A young investor might lean more towards equities for growth, while someone nearing retirement might prefer more bonds to preserve capital and generate steady income.

Bond ETFs come in various forms, including government, municipal, corporate, and international bonds, each with unique risk-return profiles.

A mix of these can further diversify your portfolio, balancing risk and return.

Factor Diversification

In real life, Factor investing is another dimension you can add to your diversification strategy.

Factors are broad, persistent drivers of returns that can include elements such as size, value, momentum, and quality. For instance, small-cap ETFs tap into the size factor, while value ETFs focus on undervalued stocks expected to perform well over time.

Implementing factor diversification helps hedge against specific risks and harness potential additional returns associated with different environment cycles.

Factor ETFs provide easy access to these strategies, allowing you to tailor your portfolio further.

Thematic Investing

Interestingly enough, Thematic ETFs have emerged as a fascinating option for investors, offering exposure to long-term trends and innovations across various industries.

Themes can range from technological advancements like artificial intelligence and clean energy to changing consumer behaviors such as e-commerce.

While thematic ETFs can offer significant growth opportunities, they also carry higher risks due to their concentration in particular trends or sectors.

Balance these buzzy opportunities with the rest of your diversified portfolio to manage the risks effectively.

Regular Portfolio Rebalancing

To maintain your diversification strategy, periodic reviewing and rebalancing of your portfolio is crucial.

This involves adjusting the weightings of your investments back to their original or desired allocation. Portfolio drift can occur due to market movements, potentially skewing your risk exposure over time.

Regular rebalancing ensures your portfolio stays aligned with your investment goals and risk tolerance.

While rebalancing frequency can vary based on personal preference or market conditions, quarterly or semi-annual reviews are standard practices among investors.

Conclusion

As strange as it sounds, Building a diversified ETF portfolio is less about complicated maneuvers and more about thoughtful construction and vigilance.

Understanding your risk tolerance, investment goals, and time horizon is paramount in selecting the appropriate diversification strategies. Core-satellite positioning, geographical and sector diversification, a balanced equity and fixed-income mix, and thematic and factor investing are tools at your disposal.

ETFs simplify the diversification process, offering exposure to broad markets, specific sectors, or unique investment themes with ease and efficiency.

By leveraging these tools, you create a strong foundation for a resilient, long-term investment portfolio, poised to capitalize on growth while mitigating risks. Building a diversified ETF portfolio is not only practical but a cornerstone to optimal investing.

Chapter 7: How to Choose the Right ETFs: Criteria and Tools for Assessment

Selecting the right Exchange Traded Funds (ETFs) is akin to crafting a symphony; it involves careful consideration, a discriminating ear for detail, and a comprehensive understanding of the instruments at your disposal.

As a burgeoning investor in the ETF market, navigating this landscape might seem daunting, but with a practical framework, you can evaluate and choose ETFs that fit your investment goals and risk appetite with confidence. This chapter provides a practical guide outlining the criteria and tools you can use to make informed decisions.

Understanding Your Investment Goals

Believe it or not, Before you even start browsing the myriad of available ETFs, you need a clear sense of your investment objectives.

Are you looking for growth, income, or a blend of both? Is preserving capital your primary concern, or are you willing to take on more risk for potentially higher returns? The clarity of your goals will guide your ETF selection process.

Investors typically aim for a mix of the following:

1. **Growth**: Focusing on capital appreciation through equities.

2. **Income**: Generating regular dividends or interest, common in bond or high-dividend equity ETFs.

Let's not forget, 3. **Diversification**: Reducing risk by spreading investments across various asset classes or sectors.

The right ETF choices should resonate with your personal goals, time horizon, and risk tolerance.

Criteria for ETF Selection

Interestingly enough, Once your investment objectives are carved in stone, it's time to delve into the specific criteria that should guide your selection:

1. **Expense Ratio**: This is one of the most crucial factors when selecting an ETF. The expense ratio represents the annual cost of holding the ETF, expressed as a percentage of your investment.

Lower expense ratios generally mean more of your money stays invested and compounds over time. While the difference between a 0. 1% and 0. 5% expense ratio might seem trivial at first glance, it can compound significantly over time.

2. **Liquidity**: An ETF's liquidity is critical, as it affects how easily you can buy or sell the ETF at your desired price.

Liquidity is largely determined by the ETF's average trading volume and the liquidity of its underlying assets. Generally, highly traded ETFs with large asset bases offer better liquidity. Smaller ETFs might have wider bid-ask spreads, increasing the cost of trading.

Let's not forget, 3. **Tracking Error**: An ETF's tracking error measures how closely the ETF follows its benchmark.

Ideally, an ETF should replicate the benchmark's performance faithfully. A significant tracking error means the ETF might be underperforming relative to its benchmark, which can defeat the purpose of your investment. Examine historical data for consistency in tracking performance.

4. **Underlying Index**: Understanding the index an ETF is tracking is imperative.

Does it align with your investment goals? Analyzing the index's composition, methodology, and sector allocations provides clarity on what you're buying. For instance, if you're interested in technology stocks, an ETF tracking the NASDAQ Composite might be suitable.

5.

Holding Details: Examine the ETF's top holdings. Are these companies or assets you're comfortable investing in? Determining if the ETF's composition is too concentrated in a few assets or sectors can help mitigate unnecessary exposure risks.

Many people don't realize this, but 6.

Dividend Yield and Payout Policy: For income-focused investors, evaluating an ETF's dividend yield and payout frequency is essential. Understanding the sustainability of these dividends, their growth potential, and how they fit into your overall income generation strategy can guide your selections.

7. **Tax Efficiency**: ETFs are generally tax-efficient investment vehicles, but variations exist.

Consider the tax implications of the capital gains distribution the ETF might incur. This is particularly relevant for investors in high tax brackets, as unnecessary distributions could erode after-tax returns.

Tools for Assessment

It's worth noting that With criteria laid out, the next step is to use the right tools to facilitate your analysis.

Several platforms and resources can help streamline your research:.

1.

ETF Screener Tools: Websites like Morningstar, ETF Database, and

Yahoo Finance offer comprehensive ETF screener tools. These tools allow you to filter ETFs based on several criteria like expense ratio, asset class, and performance, providing a customized list of ETFs that meet your specifications.

2.

Fund Fact Sheets: Every ETF provider publishes fund fact sheets detailing the ETF's performance, holdings, expense ratios, and more. These documents offer a wealth of critical information presented in a concise format, enabling you to quickly assess an ETF's credentials.

Believe it or not, 3.

Market Analysis Platforms: Platforms such as Bloomberg and Reuters offer in-depth analysis and reports on ETFs, including expert insights and market trends. These platforms can provide valuable context and foresight, aiding in making well-informed decisions.

4.

Research Reports: Financial institutions often provide research reports that analyze funds comprehensively. These reports might come with recommendations and professional ratings, which could bolster your ETF decision process.

5.

Tax Professionals and Financial Advisors: Consulting with a financial advisor or tax professional can provide personalized advice, especially if you're managing a complex portfolio or have nuanced investment or tax considerations.

Making the Final Choice

Once you've gathered all relevant information and evaluated potential ETFs through the lens of your investment criteria, the final step is integrating them into your overall investment strategy.

Ensure the ETFs complement each other, minimize overlap, and contribute positively to your portfolio's diversification.

It's also vital to keep an eye on your chosen ETFs after investing, as market conditions, expense ratios, and fund performances can change over time.

Regular portfolio reviews ensure that your ETF selections continue to align with your financial goals.

Believe it or not, By meticulously assessing ETFs using the criteria and tools outlined in this chapter, you'll be well-equipped to construct a robust, diversified, and goal-centered investment portfolio that can weather market fluctuations and build wealth over the long term.

Remember, the key to successful ETF investing isn't simply about picking the "best" funds, but about finding the right fit for your unique financial journey.

Chapter 8: The Role of Indexes in ETF Investing: A Closer Look

In the world of ETF investing, understanding the role and significance of indexes is crucial. Indexes form the backbone of most Exchange-Traded Funds (ETFs), dictating what they hold and how they're managed.

For the uninitiated, this might seem like just another layer of financial jargon. However, once you unpack the concept and see where indexes fit into the broader landscape of investment, their significance becomes clear and understandable.

At their core, indexes are simply a way to measure a specific section of the stock market. For example, the S&P 500 index tracks the performance of the 500 largest publicly traded companies in the United States. Similarly, the Dow Jones Industrial Average includes 30 significant U.

S. companies and is often cited in the media as a barometer of the broader economy. What makes indexes so vital to ETF investing is their role as benchmarks.

ETFs aim to replicate the performance of these indexes. This connection between ETFs and indexes allows investors to have a diversified hold over a segment of the market without needing to pick individual stocks.

When you invest in an ETF that tracks the S&P 500, you aren't betting on one company but the overall performance of 500 major players. This inherently spreads risk—an attractive proposition for long-term investors seeking stability.

There are a multitude of indexes catering to different sectors, markets, and themes. Industry-specific indexes might track technology, healthcare, or energy sectors, allowing you to focus your investments according to your interests or insights about certain industries.

Regional indexes might focus on emerging markets like India or Brazil, offering opportunities for those willing to venture outside domestic borders. Then there are thematic indexes that encapsulate trends such as green energy or social responsibility.

Understanding how an index is constructed is a key step for any investor. While the most common indexes are market-cap weighted, meaning the largest companies take up more space in the index, there are others that adopt equal weighting or factor-based methodologies.

Each construction method comes with its benefits and drawbacks. For example, market-cap weighting benefits from economies of scale but may overly expose investors to the largest corporations, potentially reducing diversification.

Interestingly enough, Factor-based indexes are intriguing because they take traditional elements like size and value and systematically screens them across the index.

This is often referred to as "smart beta" and offers a middle ground between passive and active investing. By understanding these unconventional methodologies, you can gain insights into sources of returns and how they fit into your investment strategy.

For those new to ETF investing, it might be tempting to follow the crowd and invest in a popular index simply because of its widespread acknowledgment and media coverage.

However, having an in-depth grasp of the underlying index's objectives and methodologies will allow you to make more informed decisions aligned with your financial aspirations.

When considering ETFs guided by an index, it's critical to evaluate how well the ETF tracks its respective index—this is known as the tracking difference.

Factors such as fund management efficiency, fees, and market conditions can create discrepancies between the index's performance and that of the ETF. The smaller the tracking error, the more reliably the ETF mirrors its index.

Interestingly enough, Moreover, even seemingly passive investments like index-tracking ETFs require active oversight to ensure they align with personal investment goals.

Factors such as changes in an index's composition or rebalancing schedules can affect the ETF's performance. Investors should monitor these developments to maintain alignment with their economic outlook and risk tolerance.

Indexes extend beyond traditional stocks.

Bond indexes, for example, track the performance of various types of fixed-income securities. These bond-focused ETFs are ideal for those seeking a conservative investment balance, as they usually exhibit lower volatility than stock-driven ETFs.

The emergence of globally focused indexes allows investors to harness opportunities beyond their home markets, diversifying geographic risk and capitalizing on the growth potential of international markets.

However, with international investments come additional factors to track, such as currency fluctuations and geopolitical risks.

Investors should be aware of indexes that blend multiple asset classes; these combination indexes may consist of elements like equities, bonds, and commodities.

ETFs following these diversified indexes simplify asset allocation and can be an excellent choice for investors aiming for a one-stop investment solution.

In summary, indexes are not just abstract numbers or arcane

measurements— they are the compass that guides ETFs.

By understanding indexes' construction, objectives, and intricacies, you not only demystify ETFs but also empower yourself to make smarter investment choices. Aligning your ETFs with the right indexes allows for a diverse, cost-effective, and relatively low-maintenance investment pathway— precisely what every long-term investor aims for when navigating the financial markets.

Being familiar with the plethora of indexes out there, their structural nuances, and the way they can influence your investment outcome is an indispensable part of mastering ETF investing.

In doing so, you move from being a passive spectator to an informed participant in the ever-evolving world of financial markets.

Chapter 9: Analyzing ETF Performance: Key Metrics and Indicators

Investing in Exchange-Traded Funds (ETFs) offers a practical solution for both novice and seasoned investors seeking diversification and potentially strong returns with a level of simplicity not as easily achievable through individual stock picking.

However, understanding how to robustly analyze ETF performance is crucial for making informed investment choices. An awareness of key metrics and performance indicators is vital in evaluating whether an ETF aligns with your financial goals.

Tracking the Benchmark

Many people don't realize this, but The first point of reference in assessing an ETF's performance is its benchmark index. ETFs are designed to track the performance of specific indices, such as the S&P 500 or the Russell 2000.

It's essential to understand not just how an ETF tracks its benchmark over time but also what factors might cause deviations from that benchmark. Such factors could include management fees, tracking error, or significant changes in the underlying index components.

Tracking error, the difference between an ETF's performance and its benchmark, is a crucial metric.

A smaller tracking error signifies that the ETF effectively replicates the index, whereas a higher tracking error may indicate issues such as inefficient portfolio management or high fund costs. A consistent tracking error analysis provides investors with insights into the reliability of an ETF relative to its stated index.

Total Return and Expense Ratio

At first glance, When evaluating ETF performance, the focus should ideally be on total return — which considers not just price appreciation but also dividend payments and capital gains distributions.

Comparing total returns of an ETF with its peers within the same asset class can clarify its competitive standing.

The expense ratio is another pivotal factor; it is the annual fee expressed as a percentage of the fund's average assets. Lower expense ratios generally enhance the investor's net return, making ETFs with minimal fees more attractive over the long term.

Keep in mind, however, that a lower expense ratio does not automatically equate to higher total performance. The balance between costs, tracking accuracy, and market exposure should guide the decision-making process.

Yield and Distribution Metrics

Many people don't realize this, but For investors seeking income-generating assets, the yield — representing the ETF's annual dividend payout divided by its current price — becomes a key measure.

Furthermore, understanding the distribution schedule and its consistency can offer insights into the stability of dividend payouts.

Payout consistency, reflected in steady or increasing distributions, suggests a resilient underlying asset pool.

Conversely, erratic payout patterns can signal underlying instability in the assets themselves. Delve deeply into historical distribution data to gauge how reliably an ETF can provide income over time.

Risk Metrics

Risk assessment plays a significant role in evaluating ETF performance. Standard deviation and Beta are two critical risk-related metrics.

Standard deviation measures the price volatility of an ETF and indicates how much an ETF's returns can vary from the mean over a set period. A higher standard deviation means more volatility and thus increased risk.

Beta, another risk parameter, measures an ETF's volatility relative to the overall market.

A Beta of 1 signifies that the ETF's price tends to move with the market, above 1 indicates more volatility than the market, and below 1 suggests less volatility. Understanding these risk parameters enables investors to match their risk tolerance with suitable ETFs.

Sharpe Ratio: Weighing Risk and Reward

The Sharpe ratio provides valuable insights into the risk-adjusted return of an ETF. Calculated by subtracting the risk-free rate of return (such as that of U.

S. Treasuries) from the ETF's return and dividing the result by its standard deviation, the Sharpe ratio helps investors ascertain whether excess returns justify the assumed risk. A higher Sharpe ratio implies better risk-adjusted performance, making it a potent tool for evaluating how well an ETF compensates for the risk taken.

Liquidity and Trading Volume

ETF liquidity, determined by average daily trading volume, is an often overlooked but critical aspect of performance assessment.

Highly liquid ETFs tend to have narrower bid-ask spreads, translating to lower transaction costs and smoother trade execution. Conversely, low liquidity could lead to wider spreads and increased slippage costs when entering or exiting a position.

I've seen this happen before: Examine an ETF's average daily volume in conjunction with its asset size.

Larger funds tend to be more liquid, but size isn't the only determinant. A detailed review of typical trading patterns versus the current conditions can offer insights into potential trading cost implications.

Tax Efficiency

One of the appealing aspects of ETFs is their tax efficiency, a byproduct of their unique structure that can result in lower capital gains distributions compared to mutual funds.

Analyze the historical capital gains distribution records to understand tax implications better. Consistent tax efficiency can significantly impact an investor's bottom line, particularly for those in higher tax brackets.

Conducting a Periodic Review

It is imperative for investors to conduct regular reviews, offering fresh perspectives on ETF performance versus initial investment theses.

Evaluate whether an ETF continues to meet your expectations, fits your risk profile, and remains aligned with your long-term financial objectives. Investment landscapes shift over time, and adaptability in response to these changes reinforces a pragmatic investment strategy.

Conclusion

Interestingly enough, Analyzing ETF performance using key metrics and indicators is an indispensable practice for constructing a robust, diversified portfolio tailored to one's financial aspirations.

By thoroughly understanding how ETFs perform vis-à-vis their benchmarks, evaluating yields and risk-adjusted returns, scrutinizing liquidity, and assessing tax implications, investors equip themselves with the essential tools for prudent decision-making. Ultimately, informed analysis fosters confidence and clarity, reinforcing the principle of simplicity that underscores ETF investment.

Chapter 10: Tax Efficiency and ETFs: Maximizing After-Tax Returns

Investing successfully involves more than choosing the right assets; it also means understanding and optimizing tax implications associated with those investments. Taxes can significantly erode your investment returns if not managed properly.

Fortunately, Exchange-Traded Funds (ETFs) are designed to be tax-efficient investment vehicles, making them an excellent choice for investors aiming to maximize after-tax returns. In this chapter, we'll explore how ETFs achieve tax efficiency, strategies to optimize your tax situation, and the practical steps you can take to ensure your investment portfolio is as tax-efficient as possible.

Understanding ETF Tax Efficiency

At first glance, ETFs have an inherent structure that tends to be more tax-efficient compared to mutual funds. The underlying mechanism that contributes to this is the creation and redemption process.

When investors buy or sell ETF shares, they do so through the stock exchange, which does not require the fund manager to liquidate holdings. This transactional methodology limits the realization of capital gains within the fund itself.

1. **In-Kind Redemptions**: Unlike mutual funds, which might need to sell securities to meet investor redemptions, ETFs typically use in-kind transactions.

This means an investor who wishes to redeem shares withdraws a pro-rata slice of the ETF's holdings, not cash. This process allows ETFs to offload stocks in a way that minimizes taxable events.

2. **Lower Turnover**: ETFs often have lower turnover compared to active mutual funds.

Lower turnover means fewer capital gains transactions are triggered, reducing the chances of taxable events. Most ETFs are designed to track an index, which inherently requires less buying and selling of securities.

At first glance, 3.

Capital Gains Distribution: Many mutual funds distribute capital gains at the end of each year, resulting in a tax event for shareholders. ETFs, because of their structure and trading methodology, tend to limit such distributions, allowing investors to defer taxes until they sell their ETF shares.

Strategies for Maximizing After-Tax Returns

Though ETFs are designed to be tax-efficient, there are additional strategies you can employ to optimize your after-tax returns.

Here's how you can leverage these strategies:.

In real life, 1. **Asset Location**: Consider your overall asset allocation and the tax implications of where you place your ETFs.

Tax-efficient investments, like ETFs that generate qualified dividends or low short-term gains, might be better suited for taxable accounts. Tax-inefficient investments, like those generating interest, are often better placed in tax-advantaged accounts like IRAs or 401(k)s.

2. **Tax-Loss Harvesting**: This strategy involves selling ETFs that have declined in value to realize capital losses.

These losses can be used to offset capital gains in other parts of your portfolio, reducing your overall taxable income. ETFs, due to their transparency and large variety, are well-suited for such activities, allowing you to replace a sold ETF with a similar but not identical fund to maintain the desired market exposure.

3.

Long-Term Holding: Maximize the benefits of lower capital gains taxes by holding ETFs for longer periods. Long-term capital gains, applicable to assets held for over a year, are taxed at a significantly lower rate than short-term gains, which are taxed at ordinary income tax rates.

Interestingly enough, 4. **Monitoring Dividend Types**: Not all ETFs distribute the same types of dividends.

Qualified dividends—those meeting specific IRS criteria—are taxed at long-term capital gains rates, which are lower than those for non-qualified dividends. Understanding the type of dividends your ETFs distribute can enhance your tax optimization efforts.

5.

Avoiding Frequent Trading: Every trade has tax implications, and frequent trading can inadvertently bump your tax bracket. Sticking to a buy-and-hold strategy minimizes short-term taxable events and aligns with the strategic nature of ETF investments.

Practical Steps to Enhance ETF Tax Efficiency

To capitalize on the tax-efficient nature of ETFs, here's what you can do:

1.

Review ETF Structure: Before investing, understand the structure of the ETF, such as whether it uses synthetic or physical replication. Ensure you are comfortable with its tax implications.

2.

IRS Forms: Use IRS Form 8949 and Schedule D to accurately report any capital gains and losses incurred from buying and selling ETFs. Correct reporting helps in managing tax efficiently.

Believe it or not, 3.

Stay Informed: Tax laws can change, and staying updated with the latest tax legislation will help you make informed investment decisions. Engaging with a tax advisor can provide tailored advice that complements your ETF investment strategy.

4.

Portfolio Rebalancing: Conduct annual or bi-annual portfolio assessments to ensure your asset allocation remains aligned with your financial goals. Use rebalancing as an opportunity to tax-loss harvest when appropriate.

5.

Utilize Technology: Numerous platforms offer tools specifically designed to help investors track tax efficiency. These tools can provide visual insights into your tax exposure and recommend tactics to mitigating tax impacts.

Conclusion

ETFs provide a robust foundation for building a tax-efficient investment portfolio. However, understanding the mechanisms that drive their efficiency enables you to better control your tax footprint and maximize your after-tax returns.

By employing smart asset placement, informed trades, and utilizing tax-smart strategies like tax-loss harvesting, you'll be well on your way to optimizing your ETF investments. Remember, while tax efficiency is important, it is one part of a comprehensive investment strategy focused on realizing long-term growth efficiently and effectively. As the financial world evolves, your awareness and proactivity in managing taxes will play a crucial role in building a prosperous investment future.

Chapter 11: Low-Cost Investing: Understanding ETF Fees and Expenses

In the realm of investments, there's a well-worn saying that echoes through the corridors of financial wisdom: "Costs matter. " Nowhere is this aphorism more palpable than in the world of Exchange-Traded Funds (ETFs).

A key allure of ETFs is their low-cost structure, a feature that turns investors' heads and draws them into the calm, rational embrace of strategic portfolio building. However, understanding the intricacies of these costs and expenses is crucial for anyone looking to maximize their investment efficiency and, ultimately, their returns. In this chapter, we will delve into the various fees and expenses associated with ETFs, explore why they matter so much, and provide you with practical advice on how to minimize them.

The Anatomy of ETF Costs

Management Fees

The primary cost associated with investing in ETFs is the management fee.

This is typically expressed as an expense ratio, a percentage of the fund's average assets under management taken annually to cover the fund's operating expenses. Unlike mutual funds, where fees are often higher due to active management strategies, ETFs tend to have lower expense ratios because many ETFs are passively managed, aiming to track an index rather than outperform it.

Expense ratios can vary significantly across the ETF landscape. Broad market ETFs often boast some of the lowest expense ratios, sometimes below 0.

10%, while more specialized or actively managed ETFs can range upwards. When considering an ETF, always check its expense ratio. A small difference in fees can have a significant impact over the long term, thanks to the power of compounding.

Trading Commissions

When you buy or sell shares of an ETF, you're subject to trading commissions, which are determined by the brokerage.

Recent industry shifts towards zero-commission trading have made this less of a concern than it once was. However, it's essential to be aware of any hidden fees that might lurk in the shadows, such as premium charges for using certain trading platforms or fees for frequent trading.

Bid-Ask Spread

Interestingly enough, A more nuanced cost is the bid-ask spread, which is the difference between the price an investor is willing to pay for an ETF (the bid) and the price at which a seller is willing to sell it (the ask). This spread can vary based on the liquidity of the ETF and the assets it holds.

Typically, more widely traded ETFs have narrower spreads, while niche or less-liquid ETFs may have wider spreads. While not a direct fee, the bid-ask spread is a hidden cost that can affect the price you pay when buying or selling ETF shares.

Hidden and Miscellaneous Costs

There are other less-visible costs that can sneak into your ETF portfolio. Securities lending is one such example.

Some ETFs lend the securities they hold to short-sellers, earning additional income. This practice can offset expenses, but it also introduces an element of risk. Additionally, currency conversion fees may apply if ETFs hold foreign assets and you're investing in a different currency.

Why Low Costs Matter

The importance of maintaining low investment costs cannot be overstated. Higher expense ratios can erode your returns over time, a phenomenon known as the "drag effect.

" This is particularly critical for long-term investors. A 1% higher annual charge might not seem significant, but imagine it applied over a 30-year investment horizon. The potential reduction in your portfolio's growth can be startlingly large.

For example, suppose you have two ETFs: ETF A with an expense ratio of 0. 10% and ETF B with an expense ratio of 1.

10%. Assuming both ETFs offer the same 7% annual return before fees, a $10,000 investment in ETF A would grow to approximately $74,872 over 30 years, while the same investment in ETF B would grow to about $57,434. That's a difference of more than $17,000, purely driven by a 1% fee differential.

Compounding Costs

Over time, the fees you pay do not just subtract from your portfolio once; they subtract again and again, reducing the overall growth potential.

This compounding effect of fees can significantly impact your long-term wealth accumulation. Therefore, paying attention to expense ratios and striving to minimize all costs associated with your investments is an exercise in fortifying your financial future.

Strategies to Minimize Costs

Choose Low-Cost ETFs

When selecting ETFs, prioritize those with the lowest possible fees, especially if they align with your investment objectives.

Many ETF providers now offer an extensive suite of ultra-low-cost funds, even for specialized sectors or niche markets. Conduct thorough research and capitalize on this abundance of options.

Beware of Turnover and Slippage

To be honest, While ETFs are generally tax-efficient due to their structure, excessive turnover within an ETF's portfolio can lead to hidden costs.

Check the turnover rate of the ETFs you are interested in and understand how it might affect potential tax obligations or transaction costs.

Utilize Commission-Free Platforms

Leverage brokerage platforms that offer commission-free ETF trading to avoid unnecessary trading costs.

Moreover, engage in practices that reduce the need to buy and sell frequently, such as adopting a long-term, buy-and-hold strategy.

Monitor Bid-Ask Spreads

Before executing trades, especially large ones, observe the ETF's bid-ask spread.

Try to execute trades during times of higher market liquidity, which typically leads to narrower spreads. Limit orders can also be used to ensure you get the price you want without falling victim to wide spreads.

Evaluate the Total Cost of Ownership

Let's not forget, In addition to expense ratios, consider all associated costs, such as bid-ask spreads, trading commissions, and even potential tax implications.

This comprehensive view helps ensure you're not overlooking significant costs that would otherwise slip under the radar.

Conclusion

Understanding ETF fees and expenses may seem daunting at first, but with a clear grasp of the basics, you're better equipped to make smarter investment choices.

By focusing on low-cost ETFs, embracing efficient trading practices, and maintaining a vigilant eye on all costs associated with your investment, you prepare yourself not only to preserve your wealth but to grow it significantly over time.

In real life, Remember, successful investing isn't just about getting the greatest returns; it's about keeping what you earn. In the long run, minimizing expenses is a powerful, time-tested strategy to help you achieve your financial goals.

As you continue this journey into ETF investing, let the principles of low-cost investing serve as your guide. They are, after all, the quiet yet steadfast guardians of your portfolio's growth.

Chapter 12: Long-Term Investment Strategies with ETFs: Setting Goals and Taking Action

Investing for the long term requires a steady hand, a stratified approach, and a keen understanding of financial instruments such as Exchange Traded Funds (ETFs).

This chapter delves deeply into how you can set effective goals and take actionable steps to build a robust, long-term investment strategy using ETFs. By the end of this chapter, you'll be equipped with practical knowledge to shape your investment goals, choose suitable ETFs, and consistently work towards a financially secure future.

Defining Your Investment Goals

It's worth noting that The starting point for any investment strategy is a clear definition of your goals.

Without this, you're akin to a sailor setting sail without a destination. Determine what you want to achieve with your investments: Are you saving for retirement, a child's education, a future purchase, or simply growing your wealth?.

Consider not just the amount of wealth you wish to accumulate, but also the timeline.

Your investment time horizon—whether it's 10, 20, or 30 years—plays a critical role in shaping your strategy. Long-term goals allow for a greater level of volatility in exchange for potentially higher returns, but they also require patience and a steadfast approach to market fluctuations.

Risk Tolerance and Asset Allocation

Many people don't realize this, but Once your goals and time frames are clear, understanding your risk tolerance becomes vital.

Your comfort with risk influences your asset allocation—the mix of equities, bonds, and other securities in your portfolio. ETFs, by nature, offer diversified exposure to various asset classes, but the specific allocation among these classes should be tailored to your risk profile.

For risk-averse investors, a larger proportion of bonds and fixed-income ETFs might be appropriate.

Conversely, those with a higher risk tolerance may lean more heavily into equities. Remember, diversification is your ally—a dispersed portfolio reduces the impact of individual asset volatility.

Selecting the Right ETFs

Choosing the right ETFs is crucial to building a portfolio aligned with your goals and risk tolerance.

Begin with broad-based index ETFs, such as those tracking the S&P 500 for equity exposure or a total bond market index for fixed-income support. These provide foundational diversification and tend to have lower fees compared to actively managed funds.

Next, consider incorporating thematic or sector-specific ETFs that align with your market outlook and values.

For example, if you believe in the growth potential of clean energy, a clean energy ETF could complement your broader portfolio. However, keep these choices balanced to prevent over-concentration in any one area.

Implementing and Monitoring Your Strategy

At first glance, With your asset allocation defined and ETFs selected, implementation involves purchasing the chosen ETFs through a brokerage account.

Be mindful of transaction fees, as they can erode your returns over time. Opt for commission-free ETF purchases when possible to optimize cost efficiency.

Long-term investing is not a set-it-and-forget-it endeavor. Regular monitoring of your portfolio ensures it remains aligned with your evolving goals.

Life events, shifts in financial circumstances, and changing market conditions may necessitate a portfolio rebalancing. This involves adjusting your allocation back to your desired levels of exposure and can prevent drift over time that might skew your risk profile.

The Discipline of Regular Investment

Many people don't realize this, but A key principle of successful long-term investing is the discipline of regular contributions. Investing consistently, regardless of market conditions, capitalizes on dollar-cost averaging.

This technique, where you invest a fixed amount at regular intervals, mitigates the impact of market volatility. You end up buying more shares when prices are low and fewer when they are high, smoothing out the average cost over time.

Automate these investments if possible.

Most brokerages offer automatic investment plans that allow funds to be deducted from your bank account and invested into your portfolio effortlessly. Automation not only takes the emotion out of investing but also enforces discipline.

Contending with Market Fluctuations

In real life, Market volatility is an inevitable aspect of investing. During periods of market downturn, it's crucial to maintain perspective.

Historically, markets have rebounded after downturns, rewarding those who stay invested for the long haul. Reacting emotionally during market dips—by selling off investments—can lock in losses and derail your long-term strategy.

Adopting a fortified mindset that views downturns as opportunities rather than threats will aid in adhering to your plan.

However, ensure your portfolio is designed to withstand these fluctuations; a well-diversified collection of ETFs spreads risk and enhances the potential for recovery.

Keeping Informed and Learning

Believe it or not, The financial world is dynamic.

Staying informed about market trends, ETF innovations, and economic shifts can provide insights into potential adjustments or opportunities within your portfolio. However, avoid the trap of information overload, which can lead to anxious decision-making.

Educational resources abound—consider books, online courses, and financial news platforms to broaden your understanding.

However, filter sources carefully to focus on quality, actionable insights rather than sensational headlines that may prompt irrational reactions.

Conclusion: Consistent Action for Long-term Success

To be honest, Building a long-term investment strategy with ETFs is a journey of patience, discipline, and informed decision-making.

Setting clear financial goals becomes the foundation upon which all other elements of your strategy are built. By understanding your risk tolerance, selecting an appropriate mix of ETFs, and committing to regular investment and portfolio review, you're well-positioned for financial success.

Remember, investing is not about making a single successful trade or timing the market perfectly.

It's about creating a coherent plan, sticking with it through market ups and downs, and making incremental adjustments as your circumstances and goals evolve. Over time, your disciplined approach will pay dividends, not just financially, but in the peace of mind that comes with a carefully curated and managed portfolio.

Chapter 13: Managing Market Volatility: Protecting Your ETF Portfolio

Investing can often feel like you're sailing across turbulent seas, with market volatility representing the unpredictable waves you must navigate.

Yet, with the right strategies and mindset, you can chart a course that protects your portfolio from unnecessary risk. In this chapter, we explore how to manage market volatility effectively, especially when dealing with Exchange-Traded Funds (ETFs).

Understanding Market Volatility

Many people don't realize this, but Before diving into strategies, it's essential to understand what market volatility is. Volatility refers to the degree of variation of a trading price series over time.

While it can offer opportunities for gains, it often evokes fear due to the potential for losses. The very nature of ETFs, which are composed of a basket of assets mirroring an index or sector, can help mitigate some individual stock risk, but it doesn't eliminate market risk entirely. Therefore, learning how to handle such fluctuations is crucial for successful investing.

Embrace a Long-Term Perspective

One of the most effective ways to manage volatility is to adopt a long-term investment approach. Historically, markets have trended upwards over the long run despite short-term fluctuations.

By focusing on long-term growth rather than short-term turmoil, you allow your investments the necessary time to recover from dips and capitalize on rebounds. When you buy ETFs and hold them over extended periods, you benefit from diversification and long-term market appreciation.

Diversification Is Key

Diversification is the cornerstone of risk management in investing. Holding a mix of different asset classes can reduce the volatility of your overall portfolio.

ETFs inherently offer diversification since they hold multiple securities. However, you still need to ensure your ETF selection represents diverse market sectors, geographies, and asset types. Mixing equities with bonds, adding some international exposure, and including sector-specific ETFs can offer a more stable performance as market conditions change.

Utilize Defensive ETFs

Defensive ETFs are designed to perform better during market downturns. These often focus on sectors that are less sensitive to economic cycles, such as utilities, consumer staples, and healthcare.

Incorporating some defensive ETFs into your portfolio can provide stability during volatile periods. Additionally, consider ETFs with a focus on dividends or low volatility, offering more consistent returns and less dramatic price swings.

Regular Review and Rebalancing

Consistent portfolio review and rebalancing are vital in managing volatility. Market fluctuations can shift your asset allocation from your original investment plan.

For instance, after a market rally, your equity allocation may exceed your risk tolerance. Conversely, market downturns might leave you with an underexposed equity position when it's a good time to buy. Rebalancing helps realign your portfolio with your initial goals, maintaining your desired risk level.

Employ Dollar-Cost Averaging

Dollar-cost averaging (DCA) is a strategy that involves investing a fixed amount of money at regular intervals, regardless of market conditions.

By doing so, you purchase more shares when prices are low and fewer when prices are high, potentially lowering your average cost per share over time. This method also reduces the pressure to time the market perfectly, a feat notoriously difficult even for seasoned investors.

Keep an Emergency Fund

Let's not forget, Having an adequate emergency fund is crucial for protecting your investment portfolio from the need for sudden withdrawals.

When unexpected expenses arise, tapping into your investments during a market downturn can lead to realized losses and negatively impact your long-term growth. An emergency fund provides a cushion and allows you to maintain your investment strategy despite short-term market upheavals.

Stay Informed, but Avoid Overreaction

Staying informed about the market environment, including economic indicators and global events, can aid in understanding potential market movements. However, it's equally important to avoid overreacting to news.

Emotional decisions driven by fear or panic often lead to selling low and buying high. Establishing an informed but measured approach helps maintain rational decision-making in the face of market volatility.

Consider Professional Guidance

If managing market volatility seems overwhelming, consider engaging with a financial advisor.

A professional can help you devise and adhere to a strategy that aligns with your financial goals and risk tolerance. They provide expert insights and emotional discipline, aiding you to stay on course amidst volatility.

Conclusion: Navigating Volatility with Confidence

Navigating market volatility requires a blend of strategic diversification, disciplined planning, and a steady mental approach. By keeping your focus on long-term objectives, diversifying your investments with well-chosen ETFs, and embracing strategies like dollar-cost averaging and regular rebalancing, you can protect your portfolio from the harshest impacts of market adversity.

Remember, successful investing is as much about managing risks as it is about seeking returns. By incorporating these practices, you're better positioned to sail through turbulent times with confidence and optimism.

Chapter 14: The Psychology of Investing: Overcoming Emotional Decisions

Investing in Exchange-Traded Funds (ETFs) offers an excellent opportunity for long-term growth with the convenience of simplicity. However, even the most disciplined investors can fall prey to the psychological pitfalls of emotional decision-making.

Understanding the underlying psychology of investing can help you maintain a steady hand, especially during market fluctuations. This chapter aims to unravel the complex web of emotions that influence investment decisions and provide practical strategies to overcome them.

Understanding Emotional Triggers

In real life, Investing is as much an emotional endeavor as it is a financial one. The markets are often volatile, testing the emotional resilience of investors.

Emotional triggers such as fear, greed, overconfidence, and regret can lead even the savviest of investors astray. Recognizing these emotions is the first step to managing them.

1. **Fear and Panic**: Fear is one of the most potent emotions in investing.

It often manifests during market downturns, pushing investors to make impulsive decisions like selling their holdings at a loss. During such times, it's important to remember that markets are cyclical and downturns are often followed by recoveries.

2. **Greed and Overconfidence**: On the flip side, during market upswings, greed and overconfidence can lead investors to take unnecessary risks.

The fear of missing out (FOMO) can drive decisions to chase high returns through speculative investments. This approach often results in buying at the peak of the market.

Many people don't realize this, but 3. **Loss Aversion and Regret**: Humans tend to feel the pain of losses more acutely than the pleasure of gains.

This can lead to holding onto losing investments for too long, hoping they will rebound, or selling winning investments too early to "lock in gains. " Regret over past decisions can cloud judgment, influencing future choices.

Strategies to Overcome Emotional Investing

Develop a Robust Investment Plan

It's worth noting that Creating and adhering to a well-thought-out investment plan serves as a buffer against emotional impulses.

Your investment strategy should be built around clear goals, risk tolerance, and an understanding of market behavior. This plan should guide your decisions, keeping them aligned with long-term objectives rather than short-term emotions.

Actionable Tip: Write down your investment goals and the specific strategies to achieve them.

Refer to this plan during volatile market periods to remind yourself of the bigger picture.

Set and Forget

Once you've created a diversified ETF portfolio that aligns with your objectives, adopt a 'set and forget' approach.

Frequent monitoring of the market can exacerbate emotional responses. Trust in your strategy and let the power of compounding work in your favor over time.

Actionable Tip: Schedule regular, but infrequent, portfolio review dates — quarterly or bi-annually. This reduces the temptation to react to short-term market movements.

Implement Stop-Loss Orders

I’ve seen this happen before: Incorporating stop-loss orders into your strategy can help prevent emotional decisions during market fluctuations.

By setting predetermined price points to sell an asset, you limit potential losses without having to make a decision in the heat of the moment.

Actionable Tip: Based on your risk tolerance, decide on a specific percentage loss that you can bear for each ETF in your portfolio.

Use stop-loss orders to automate this process.

Use Dollar-Cost Averaging

It’s worth noting that Dollar-cost averaging is a disciplined investing approach that involves regularly buying fixed amounts of an investment, regardless of its price.

This strategy mitigates the risk of timing the market and reduces the impact of volatility on your portfolio.

Actionable Tip: Set up automatic monthly deposits into your ETF investment account.

This helps you to consistently invest through market highs and lows, smoothing out purchase price over time.

Educate Yourself

Knowledge is a powerful antidote to fear and greed.

By deepening your understanding of market principles and the assets in your portfolio, you can build the confidence needed to trust your decisions amidst the noise.

Actionable Tip: Dedicate time each month to read books, articles, or attend workshops on investing.

The more informed you are, the less likely you are to make emotional decisions.

Mindfulness and Reflection

To be honest, Practicing mindfulness can help maintain composure during periods of market volatility.

Take time to reflect on your emotional responses and understand their root causes. This self-awareness can help you recognize emotional impulses before they affect your investment decisions.

Actionable Tip: Start a journal where you document your thoughts and emotions during market moves.

Review these entries to identify patterns and triggers that lead to impulsive actions.

Building the Right Mindset

As strange as it sounds, A successful investor is not devoid of emotions but understands how to manage them.

Developing a resilient mindset is critical for long-term investing success. This means embracing patience, staying disciplined, and focusing on process rather than outcomes.

1.

Acceptance: Accept that market fluctuations are a natural part of investing. By viewing volatility as an opportunity rather than a threat, you can reframe your emotional responses to market changes.

2.

Long-term Focus: Keep your eyes on the ultimate prize: your long-term financial goals. By maintaining a future-oriented perspective, you can rise above the noise of daily market movements.

To be honest, 3.

Process over Results: Focus on the quality of your decision-making process, not just the results. A good decision is informed, rational, and aligned with your investment plan, regardless of the short-term outcome.

4. **Self-compassion**: It's inevitable to make mistakes along the way.

Treat yourself with the same kindness and understanding you would offer a friend. Learn from your mistakes, and use them as stepping stones toward better decision-making.

Conclusion

As strange as it sounds, The intersection of psychology and investing is a complex yet fascinating domain. By recognizing emotional triggers and implementing practical strategies, you can shield your investment decisions from the whims of emotions.

ETF investing, with its emphasis on diversification and simplicity, is an ideal vehicle for applying these principles effectively. By building an emotional toolkit and developing a resilient mindset, you're not just investing in ETFs, but in your own growth as a disciplined, long-term investor.

Chapter 15: Common Mistakes in ETF Investing and How to Avoid Them

Investing has always been a realm where the wise and informed tend to outperform the impulsive and uninformed. Exchange-traded funds (ETFs), while inherently simpler than many other investment vehicles, come with their own set of pitfalls.

As investors seek the balance of risk and return in their portfolio designs, understanding common mistakes in ETF investing and how to avoid them is paramount. In this chapter, we'll delve into missteps often made by both novice and seasoned investors and provide practical guidance to shield you from these pitfalls.

Mistake #1: Overlooking Fundamentals

Interestingly enough, One of the cardinal sins in ETF investing is neglecting to understand the fundamental principle behind the ETF. Many investors are blinded by past performance stats without comprehending the underlying assets that constitute an ETF.

It's essential to delve into the composition of any ETF before investing. Scrutinize the sectors and companies that make up the fund. Just because an ETF has had high returns in the past does not mean its future will be equally bright if its underlying fundamentals do not support that growth.

Avoidance Strategy: Prioritize understanding over performance.

Utilize resources that provide comprehensive information about the ETF's holdings, sector weightings, and overall investment approach. Use this information to judge whether an ETF aligns with your financial goals and risk tolerance.

Mistake #2: Ignoring Costs

As strange as it sounds, The allure of low-cost investing is a primary reason many flock to ETFs.

However, the misconception that all ETFs are created equal in terms of expense ratios can lead to costly misjudgments. While most ETFs offer a cost-effective approach relative to mutual funds, differences in expense ratios and other hidden fees can impact your net returns over time.

Avoidance Strategy: Always check the expense ratio of an ETF. It may seem minor, but as these fees accumulate, they can eat significantly into long-term returns.

Compare similar ETFs to find the one that offers the best balance between cost and expected performance. Assess embedded costs like bid-ask spreads and trading commissions when calculating the true cost of an ETF.

Mistake #3: Excessive Trading

At first glance, The liquidity of ETFs makes them an attractive and flexible tool for many investors.

However, this very liquidity can seduce some investors into a pattern of excessive trading. Day trading or frequent buying and selling of ETFs can lead to high transaction costs and tax inefficiencies, possibly negating the benefits of using ETFs.

Avoidance Strategy: Adopt a disciplined long-term investment strategy. Set clear investment goals and time horizons, and stick to them.

Avoid the temptation of market timing, which is often unpredictable and risky. An intermittent portfolio rebalancing strategy is fine; however, it should be done within the context of long-term goals, not short-term gains.

Mistake #4: Lack of Diversification

I've seen this happen before: Even though ETFs inherently provide diversification by encompassing a range of securities, relying solely on a single or limited number of ETFs can lead to overexposure to similar risks.

A lack of diversification defeats one of the core benefits ETFs offer.

Avoidance Strategy: Diversify your choice of ETFs across different asset classes, sectors, and geographic regions.

Construct a portfolio that includes a mix of equity, bond, and specialty ETFs to spread risk more effectively. Ensure that your portfolio aligns with your investment goals and risk tolerance without heavy concentration in one area.

Mistake #5: Overemphasis on Dividend Yields

High dividend yield ETFs can be enticing, especially in low-interest-rate environments.

However, focusing exclusively on yield can lead to investments in funds with companies that are less stable or take on excessive debt to finance dividends.

Avoidance Strategy: Evaluate dividend yield alongside other factors like the growth prospects of the companies within the ETF.

Utilize total return analysis—considering both dividend yields and capital gains—to gain a holistic view of the ETF's performance potential.

Mistake #6: Ignoring Tax Implications

I've seen this happen before: ETFs are generally tax-efficient, but that does not mean they're immune to taxes.

Capital gains distributions and dividends can incur tax consequences, impacting the returns on taxable accounts.

Avoidance Strategy: Be proactive in understanding the tax implications of your ETF investments. Consider the type of account—taxable vs.

tax-advantaged—and invest accordingly. For taxable accounts, focus on ETFs that have a history of minimal capital gain distributions. Furthermore, consult with a tax advisor for tailored advice, especially regarding tax-advantaged strategies like tax-loss harvesting.

Mistake #7: Following the Herd

Let's not forget, The buzz around certain ETFs can lead investors to follow trends rather than research-based decisions.

This herd mentality can result in buying high and selling low—a recipe for poor returns.

Avoidance Strategy: Engage in thorough research and base your investment decisions on personal financial objectives and risk assessments rather than market hype.

Develop a well-thought-out investment plan tailored to your needs and stick to it, making decisions based on data rather than emotion.

Conclusion

As strange as it sounds, ETF investing, when executed with mindfulness of common missteps, can serve as a potent component of a diversified and robust portfolio. By taking the time to understand underlying fundamentals, cost structures, diversification, tax implications, and avoiding the pitfalls of excessive trading or herd mentality, you can enhance your portfolio's long-term performance.

Ultimately, the responsibility lies in aligning your strategy with your financial goals and risk tolerance, exercising patience, and seeking continual education in an ever-evolving financial landscape. In doing so, you can circumvent the common mistakes that many investors fall victim to and harness the full potential of ETFs for your long-term financial success.

Chapter 16: Navigating Financial Crises: ETFs During Market Turbulence

When financial markets experience turbulence, the air can become thick with panic and uncertainty. Rising volatility, plummeting prices, and grim headlines can easily unsettle even the most seasoned investors.

It is during these times that Exchange-Traded Funds (ETFs) shine, not just surviving market upheavals but often thriving as investors seek the balance of diversification and liquidity that ETFs uniquely offer. In this chapter, we will delve into the role of ETFs during financial crises and how they can be harnessed to weather economic storms confidently.

Understanding Market Turbulence

In real life, Before diving into strategies, it is crucial to understand what constitutes market turbulence.

Financial crises come in various forms—global recessions, regional economic collapses, or industry-specific downturns—but they share a common characteristic: high volatility and uncertainty that cause rapid asset price declines.

History has no shortage of examples: the 2008 Global Financial Crisis, the Dot-Com bubble burst, or the more recent COVID-19 pandemic-induced market crash.

Each offered lessons in risk, resilience, and recovery. Amidst such chaos, the predictability and ease of use that ETFs offer become key benefits to investors.

The Resilience of ETFs in Crises

Many people don't realize this, but ETFs, owing to their structure, provide certain advantages during market turbulence:

1.

Instant Diversification: By their nature, ETFs are baskets of multiple securities, which can include stocks, bonds, commodities, or other financial assets. This intrinsic diversification helps mitigate the risk that comes with holding individual stocks, especially when certain sectors are hit harder than others during a crisis.

2.

Liquidity: Unlike mutual funds that settle their trades at the end of the day, ETFs trade on exchanges like individual stocks, offering intraday liquidity. This means that even during volatile periods, investors can react quickly to market dynamics, which can be crucial during fast-moving financial crises.

Many people don't realize this, but 3.

Cost Efficiency: In turbulent markets, the low-cost nature of ETFs provides an edge. With expense ratios generally lower than mutual funds and no sales loads, the transaction costs in choppy markets do not eat into returns as significantly.

4.

Transparency: Most ETFs publicly disclose their holdings daily, offering peace of mind to investors who want to understand precisely what they own, unlike mutual funds which typically disclose assets on a quarterly basis.

5.

Tax Efficiency: Thanks to their unique creation and redemption mechanism involving in-kind transactions, ETFs can often avoid triggering capital gains taxes, preserving more wealth for investors over time.

Strategies for Using ETFs During Crises

Being prepared is perhaps the most essential strategy in crisis management. Here are some steps to consider when using ETFs to navigate market turbulence:

1. **Review Your Asset Allocation**: Before crises hit, review your asset allocation.

Diversifying across asset classes—stocks, bonds, sectors, and geographies—can buffer against market shocks. For instance, if stocks plummet, having some exposure to bond ETFs, which often act as a counterweight, can stabilize your portfolio.

I've seen this happen before: 2. **Use Sector and Thematic ETFs**: During crises, some sectors may perform well while others suffer.

Sector-specific ETFs allow you to overweight or underweight particular industries based on your analysis or evolving economic conditions. Thematic ETFs focusing on trends such as cybersecurity or clean energy can also offer opportunities for growth during recoveries.

3.

Consider Defensive ETFs: Some ETFs are designed for defensive strategies. These may focus on sectors like utilities or consumer staples, which tend to be more stable during economic downturns because they cater to ongoing essential needs.

4.

Keep Cash Reserves with Short-Duration Bond ETFs: Holding some low-risk, short-duration bond ETFs can provide liquidity and minimal risk exposure. In a market downturn, they offer relatively stable returns and can be held as cash reserves until it's safe to reinvest in growth-oriented assets.

As strange as it sounds, 5.

Control Emotions Through Automatic Investments: Use automated investment strategies such as dollar-cost averaging (DCA), where you invest a fixed amount at regular intervals. This mitigates the impact of volatility by purchasing more shares when prices are low and fewer when prices are high, keeping emotions at bay when market signals are confusing.

Real-Life Applications

Consider the 2008 financial crisis.

Investors holding a diversified portfolio of equity and bond ETFs fared better than those heavily invested in individual stocks. Similarly, during the COVID-19 pandemic, while broad market indexes initially nosedived, ETFs offering exposure to technology and health sectors found resilience and growth opportunities.

One key success story is that of an investor with a balanced portfolio using a variety of ETFs across global equities, sectors, and bonds, who not only cushioned their downturn losses but also positioned their portfolio for robust recovery.

By the time markets rebounded, such a diversified strategy enabled significant gains over those who panicked and moved to cash.

Final Thoughts

While financial crises can unsettle markets, understanding and utilizing the versatility of ETFs transforms potential liabilities into opportunities.

Armed with the right knowledge and approach, investors can effectively use ETFs to shield their portfolios from the full brunt of market upheavals and emerge stronger in the long-term.

In real life, Remember, the hallmark of a successful investor is not just how they perform during boom times but how they navigate the inevitable busts.

With ETFs as part of your investment toolbox, you hold a pragmatic and powerful resource to protect and grow your wealth—through calm and storm alike.

Chapter 17: Sustainable and Ethical Investing: ESG and Themed ETFs

In the evolving landscape of investing, growing awareness of social and environmental issues has given rise to a focus on sustainable and ethical investment strategies.

For modern investors, achieving financial growth while aligning with personal values is increasingly significant. Enter Environmental, Social, and Governance (ESG) and Themed ETFs—innovative solutions that allow investors to support causes they care about while enjoying the benefits of diversification, liquidity, and simplicity that come with ETF investing.

Understanding ESG Investing

ESG investing involves selecting companies based on their performance in key areas: environmental impact, social responsibility, and governance practices. Environmental criteria consider how a company performs as a steward of nature, which includes factors like resource management, emissions, and environmental protection policies.

Social criteria examine how it manages relationships with employees, suppliers, customers, and the communities where it operates. Governance focuses on a company's leadership, executive pay, audits, internal controls, and shareholder rights.

Investors interested in ESG funds aren't just satisfied with profitable companies; they seek those that actively engage in positive ethical practices.

This approach not only aims for financial return but also contributes towards sustainable societal impact.

What are Themed ETFs?

Themed ETFs dive deeper, targeting specific investment themes or global trends such as renewable energy, clean technology, or gender equality.

These funds selectively invest in companies directly related to a particular theme, granting investors exposure to niche markets or cutting-edge industries.

While both ESG and Thematic ETFs serve to drive positive change, Themed ETFs often focus on broader concepts and may not comprehensively address all ESG criteria.

This makes themed ETFs an ideal choice for those keen on supporting specific innovations or sectors, like solar energy or blockchain technology.

Why Consider ESG and Themed ETFs?

Interestingly enough, The compelling advantage of these ETFs is their dual offering of meaningful investing and solid financial returns. Here's why you might consider them:

1.

Access to Growing Markets: ESG and thematic areas, such as clean energy or social justice, often represent early stages of ongoing megatrends. As global interest towards sustainability grows, so does the market cap of such sectors, potentially leading to attractive long-term returns.

2.

Risk Mitigation: Companies adhering to high ESG standards often display resilience against regulatory fines, reputational damage, and operational risks. By investing in such ETFs, you are lessening exposure to companies that might face climate-related transitions or societal backlash.

Many people don't realize this, but 3.

Portfolio Diversification: ESG and Themed ETFs enable diversification into industries and sectors that traditional investments might overlook, making them an effective way to round out a portfolio.

4.

Alignment with Values: Beyond financial gain, ethical investing allows you to support initiatives that match your values. It's an opportunity to contribute to global challenges like climate change, equality, and corporate responsibility.

Selecting the Right ESG or Themed ETFs

Believe it or not, When choosing an ESG or Themed ETF, multiple factors should guide your decision:

- **ETF Composition:** Know the criteria that an ETF uses for stock selection.

Assess its holdings to ensure they align with your ethical objectives. Transparency is key, so favor funds with clear methodologies and detailed reporting on ESG criteria.

- **Performance:** While past performance isn't a guarantee of future results, examining historical performance can provide insights.

Look for consistency and how the fund has managed both booms and downturns.

As strange as it sounds, - **Expense Ratios:** As with any investment, fees and expense ratios matter.

Higher-than-average expenses can eat into returns, so consider cost-effective options that balance fees with performance.

- **Impact Reporting:** A fund's capability to showcase its impact through reporting is crucial.

These reports outline the tangible outcomes achieved by the companies within the ETF, exemplifying their alignment with your ethical aims.

Strategies for Incorporating ESG/ Themed ETFs in Your Portfolio

>**Balanced Approach:** Start by complementing your traditional investment portfolio with ESG or Themed ETFs. Consider sector exposure and geographic diversification when adding these funds.

>**Core-Satellite Strategy:** Use ESG or Themed ETFs majorly as satellite additions to your core holdings, especially for diversifying into emerging sectors without excessive risk concentration.

>**Regular Reassessment:** ESG practices and trends evolve, so it's essential to stay updated on changes within your ETFs.

Regularly evaluate your positions to ensure they still align with both your financial and ethical goals.

Challenges and Considerations

While promising, ESG and Themed ETFs come with their share of challenges:

- **Greenwashing Risk:** Some companies might overstate their commitment to ESG principles for marketing purposes without substantial action behind their claims.

Thus, conducting due diligence is crucial.

To be honest, - **Evolving Standards:** ESG criteria and thematic trends are continuously maturing, but standardization is lacking.

Different funds have varying definitions and scopes, necessitating careful consideration before investment.

- **Performance Risks:** Depending too heavily on niche markets might lead to volatility.

Themed ETFs, especially, can be subject to hype risk where sectors experience unsustainable growth followed by corrections.

Conclusion

As strange as it sounds, ESG and Themed ETFs offer a pragmatic pathway to harmonize financial goals with personal values. They allow conscientious investors to make informed choices not just for returns but for positive environmental and social impact alongside.

With the right approach, diligent research, and awareness of inherent challenges, these investment vehicles can serve as meaningful components of a robust, diversified portfolio. Remember that while investing with your conscience is rewarding, maintaining a balanced, informed strategy is critical to long-term success.

Chapter 18: Technological Tools for ETF Investors: From Research to Execution

As an investor navigating the world of exchange-traded funds (ETFs), leveraging technology can be your greatest ally.

With the click of a button, you can access an array of tools designed to research, analyze, and execute investments efficiently. This chapter aims to guide you through these technological resources, transforming what might seem like a complex landscape into an accessible and efficient investment journey.

Research: Laying the Groundwork

Let's not forget, The foundation of any solid investment strategy is thorough research.

Here is where technology shines, providing platforms that offer an abundance of data and insights.

Online Investment Platforms

Platforms like Morningstar, Bloomberg, and Yahoo Finance are goldmines of information.

They provide detailed analyses, historical performance data, and expert commentary on a variety of ETFs. For instance, Morningstar offers ratings based on risk-adjusted performance, helping you compare ETFs and assess their potential alignment with your risk tolerance and investment goals.

ETF Research Tools and Screeners

ETF screening tools are invaluable for narrowing down options based on your specific criteria. Websites like ETF.

com offer powerful screeners where you can filter thousands of ETFs based on factors such as asset class, performance, expense ratio, and geographical exposure. These tools simplify the process of discovering ETFs that fit your investment strategy, saving you hours of manual research.

Robo-Advisors

To be honest, Robo-advisors like Betterment, Wealthfront, and Vanguard Personal Advisor Services provide automated portfolio management based on your risk tolerance and financial goals.

These platforms use sophisticated algorithms to suggest diversified ETF portfolios. They are ideal for investors seeking a hands-off approach, integrating technology to balance your portfolio with minimal human intervention.

Analysis: Understanding Your Investment

Once you have a shortlist of potential ETFs, the next step is analysis.

Here, technology plays a crucial role in helping you understand potential investments in detail.

Portfolio Analysis Tools

Platforms like Personal Capital and Morningstar's Portfolio Manager allow you to analyze your current portfolio, offering insights into asset allocation, sector exposure, and risk profile.

These tools often integrate with multiple brokerage accounts, giving you a comprehensive view of your investments' performance.

Risk Assessment Tools

Let's not forget, Understanding risk is vital in any investment strategy.

Tools like Riskalyze help investors assess the risk associated with specific ETFs. By inputting your desired risk tolerance, these platforms can gauge whether your ETF choices align with your financial comfort zone, helping you avoid unwanted surprises in volatile markets.

Tax Impact Analysis

Tax efficiency is an often overlooked yet crucial aspect of investing.

Tools like H&R Block and TurboTax offer tax optimization services, providing insights into potential tax implications of your ETF trades. They help ensure that your investment returns are maximized by keeping tax liabilities in check—a critical advantage for long-term compounding.

Execution: Making the Trade

Once you have done your research and analysis, it's time to execute your trades. Technology simplifies this process significantly.

Online Brokerage Platforms

Many people don't realize this, but Online brokerages like Charles Schwab, Fidelity, and E*TRADE offer platforms where you can buy and sell ETFs with ease.

They provide a seamless interface for executing trades, setting limit orders, and automating purchases. Additionally, many brokerages offer commission-free ETF trades, reducing transaction costs and boosting overall returns.

Mobile Trading Apps

Mobile apps have revolutionized the way we invest, providing all the features of online brokerage platforms in the palm of your hand.

Apps such as Robinhood or TD Ameritrade's mobile trading app allow you to stay connected to the market wherever you are. Real-time notifications on market conditions, dividend payouts, and trade execution coming to your mobile device mean you'll never miss an opportunity.

Automated Rebalancing Tools

To maintain an optimal portfolio, regular rebalancing is necessary. This involves adjusting your holdings to reclaim your initial asset allocation.

Automated rebalancing tools, like those offered by Wealthfront, make this task effortless. These tools periodically adjust your portfolio's allocation without your intervention, ensuring your investments remain aligned with your goals over time.

Future Trends: AI and Machine Learning in ETF Investing

Looking ahead, artificial intelligence (AI) and machine learning are poised to further transform ETF investing.

Platforms are increasingly incorporating AI to provide more personalized portfolio suggestions based on nuanced data points, like behavioral metrics and market sentiment analysis. As these technologies evolve, they will offer even more tailored investment solutions, empowering investors to make data-driven decisions with greater accuracy and confidence.

Practical Tips for Leveraging Technology

1. **Stay Updated**: Financial markets are dynamic. Subscribing to ETF reports and notifications from investment platforms keeps you informed about the latest trends and analytics.

Let's not forget, 2.

Use Educational Resources: Many platforms offer free educational content, webinars, and tutorials. Regularly enhance your knowledge to make the most of technological tools at your disposal.

3.

Test Before Committing: Many tools offer trial periods or free versions. Use these opportunities to evaluate whether a service aligns with your investment process before making financial commitments.

4. **Data Security**: With great power comes great responsibility.

Ensure that any platform or tool you use employs robust security measures. Enable two-factor authentication and regularly update passwords to protect your investment accounts.

Interestingly enough, In conclusion, technology has become an indispensable companion for ETF investors, simplifying processes from research to execution.

By integrating these tools into your investment strategy, you can enhance efficiency, improve decision-making, and ultimately craft a streamlined path toward your financial goals. As this technology landscape continues to expand, staying informed and adaptable will ensure that you, as an investor, capitalize on these advancements to secure a prosperous financial future.

Chapter 19: Future Trends in ETF Investing: What to Watch For

As we look towards the future of exchange-traded funds (ETFs), it's clear that this dynamic investment vehicle continues to revolutionize the way investors build their portfolios. With its potential for diversification, cost efficiency, and accessibility, the ETF landscape is poised for even more growth and innovation.

However, like any evolving market, it's crucial for investors to stay abreast of emerging trends to strategically position themselves. This chapter delves into the key trends expected to shape the future of ETF investing and what this means for your portfolio.

Expanding Thematic ETFs

At first glance, One of the most noticeable trends in ETF investing is the rise of thematic ETFs.

These funds focus on specific investment themes or sectors, such as technology, climate change, or social good. Driven by investors' growing desire to align investments with personal values or capitalize on future growth opportunities, thematic ETFs have gained traction.

As the world embraces trends like artificial intelligence, renewable energy, and biotechnology, thematic ETFs allow investors to capture the growth of these burgeoning sectors. Watch for continued expansion in niche areas.

Companies launching ETFs will continue to cater to an increasingly diverse range of interests and innovations, offering retail investors unprecedented access to emerging sectors. The key to investing in thematic ETFs is thorough research; ensure the theme aligns with your risk tolerance and long-term objectives.

Sustainable and ESG Investing

Interestingly enough, Environmental, social, and governance (ESG) investing is no longer a fringe movement. It's becoming mainstream.

ESG-focused ETFs concentrate on investments in companies that demonstrate strong governance practices, social responsibility, and environmental sustainability. This drive towards conscientious capitalism means a burgeoning market for sustainable ETFs, reflecting a changing ethos in how we perceive corporate responsibility.

As ESG investing grows, so will the range of available products and the competitiveness on performance metrics. For investors, understanding the nuances of ESG ratings and methodologies is essential.

Look not just at performance, but at the sincerity and depth of the ESG criteria ETFs claim to meet. In a world demanding accountability and transparency, investors have the power to promote change through their capital, making ESG ETFs a compelling option for those looking to merge financial returns with social impact.

Increased Adoption of Smart Beta Strategies

At first glance, Smart beta strategies offer another exciting area of development within ETFs.

Traditional market-cap weighting gives way to factors like value, momentum, and volatility. These strategies aim to deliver better risk-adjusted returns than traditional passive management.

In the future, anticipate more sophisticated versions of smart beta ETFs as firms respond to investor demand for products that outperform broader markets without stepping entirely into active management.

Exploring these offerings can introduce complexity, but for those who want to exploit specific market dynamics or reduce volatility, smart beta ETFs could be a valuable addition to a diverse portfolio.

Technological Advances and Digital Platforms

Believe it or not, The ongoing digital revolution continues to make investing more accessible and efficient.

Online platforms offering zero-commission trades and robo-advisors employing complex algorithms to recommend tailored ETF portfolios are just the beginning. As technology advances, expect integration with big data and machine learning to offer even more personalized investment solutions.

Investors should leverage these tools to gain insights into ETF performance, rebalance portfolios based on predictive analytics, and streamline their investment processes.

The key is to remain adaptable and curious about how technology can revolutionize ETF investing while ensuring that the human oversight of one's investment strategy remains a priority.

Rising Interest in Global and Emerging Markets

Let's not forget, With domestic markets reaching saturation, investors are looking toward global and emerging markets for growth opportunities.

ETFs make it relatively easy to gain exposure to these areas, offering access to regions and sectors that may have been inaccessible to retail investors in the past.

In the coming years, expect an expansion in offerings focused on these markets. Pay attention to geopolitical risks and currency fluctuations, which can add layers of complexity.

The potential rewards of diversifying globally can be significant, but they require careful analysis. Seek out ETFs that offer diversified exposure to regions showing resilience and growth potential while balancing potential risks with your overall portfolio strategy.

Regulatory Evolutions

Interestingly enough, The ETF market continues to attract significant attention from regulators worldwide.

This scrutiny stems from the growing popularity and complexity of these investment vehicles. While regulations could introduce constraints, they also provide an added layer of safety and transparency for investors.

Stay informed about regulatory changes that may impact the ETF industry.

Whether it's new rules governing disclosure or listing requirements, being aware will allow you to react strategically, ensuring your investments remain aligned with both compliance standards and your financial goals.

Conclusion: Navigating Tomorrow's ETF Landscape Today

The future of ETF investing is shaped by innovation and a deeper alignment with investor values and technology.

With thematic investments, ESG criteria, smart beta tactics, digital innovations, global diversification, and regulatory oversight all playing pivotal roles, the landscape ahead presents a rich tapestry of opportunities and challenges.

As a practical investor, your task is to distill these trends into actionable insights fitting your personal financial goals, risk tolerance, and timelines.

Keeping abreast of these developments while grounded in a long-term strategy will help you navigate the evolving ETF landscape effectively. By staying informed and adaptable, you can build a portfolio that not only capitalizes on current trends but also prospers in the ever-evolving future of ETF investing.

Chapter 20: Conclusion: Simplifying the Path to Financial Independence with ETFs

As we conclude our journey through the intricacies and opportunities of ETF investing, it's essential to take a step back and appreciate the simplicity and power of Exchange-Traded Funds as a tool for achieving financial independence.

ETFs have revolutionized the way individuals approach investing by offering a straightforward path to a diversified, balanced, and cost-effective portfolio. In this final chapter, let's distill the key lessons learned and solidify your understanding of how ETFs can serve as a reliable cornerstone for your financial future.

Embracing Simplicity and Diversity

To be honest, The allure of ETFs lies in their ability to streamline investing into a manageable endeavor without sacrificing the crucial element of diversification.

Unlike picking individual stocks, which requires in-depth research and an understanding of complex market dynamics, ETFs allow you to effortlessly gain exposure to a broad market spectrum. Whether your goal is to invest in the S&P 500, capture emerging market growth, or access bonds for risk mitigation, there's likely an ETF designed for your specific interests.

By curating your portfolio with a blend of various ETFs, you inherently diversify your investments across multiple sectors, industries, and geographic regions.

This diversification minimizes unsystematic risk—the kind tied to individual companies or specific sectors—and instead aligns your potential gains with the performance of broader market segments.

Cost-Effectiveness: The Silent Wealth Builder

As strange as it sounds, Costs are often an underestimated factor eroding long-term investment returns. ETFs are known for their low expense ratios compared to mutual funds, making them a more cost-effective choice for many investors.

With fewer fees depleting your capital, more of your money remains invested and able to compound over time—what Einstein famously referred to as the "eighth wonder of the world. ".

Trading efficiency further compounds the cost advantages.

ETFs provide the flexibility to trade throughout the day at market prices, unlike mutual funds that settle at end-of-day net asset values. This liquidity allows for strategic adjustments without the penalty of costly loads or redemption fees associated with some mutual funds, thus keeping the momentum of your wealth-building efforts intact.

Transparency and Control

To be honest, ETFs stand out for their transparency. Investors can easily access information about an ETF's holdings, typically updated daily.

This transparency ensures that you're always informed about what you own, allowing for strategic rebalancing as your financial situation or market conditions change. Unlike some investment vehicles where holdings and strategies may be opaque, ETFs provide clarity, enabling you to maintain greater control over your financial destiny.

Having control over your portfolio is empowering.

With ETFs, you decide the level of risk you're comfortable with and the investment themes or values you wish to emphasize. Whether you're focusing on sustainable investments, sector-specific plays, or adhering to classic index strategies, ETFs offer the control necessary for personalized portfolio management.

Keeping Emotion at Bay

It's worth noting that The emotional aspect of investing cannot be ignored.

Market volatility can tempt even seasoned investors to react impulsively. ETFs, with their diverse holdings and broad market strategies, act as a buffer against the emotional rollercoaster, encouraging a focus on long-term trends rather than short-term fluctuations.

By adhering to a structured investment plan that involves regular contributions to a portfolio made up of diversified ETFs, you safeguard against emotional decisions that can erode wealth.

Dollar-cost averaging, for instance, is a simple strategy that leverages regular investment contributions to smooth out market highs and lows. This disciplined approach aligns well with the inherent design of ETFs, helping maintain focus on your end goal: financial independence.

Long-Term Vision and Commitment

Financial independence is a long-term goal, requiring patience, commitment, and consistent effort. ETFs provide the framework for such disciplined investing.

Establish a routine of regular contributions to your ETF portfolio to maximize growth opportunities through compounding. As your circumstances evolve, so too can your investment strategy. Rebalancing your ETF allocations periodically is essential to ensure alignment with your evolving financial goals and risk tolerance.

Understanding the tax implications of ETF investments is also pivotal.

Many ETFs are tax-efficient due to their structural ability to minimize capital gains distributions. However, being aware of how taxes affect your returns, especially in taxable accounts, is part of maintaining a healthy, long-term investment strategy.

The Road Ahead

To be honest, With the groundwork laid, the road to financial independence using ETFs is indeed simplified.

The key is to remain informed, disciplined, and adaptable. Economic climates may change, and market dynamics may shift, but a robust ETF strategy can withstand variability and propel you towards your financial goals with confidence.

As you continue on this investment journey, remember that complexity is not synonymous with success.

Embrace the simplicity, adaptability, and prowess of ETFs to keep your investment path clear and focused. Understand your financial goals deeply, remain steadfast in your strategies, and let the benefits of ETF investing guide you toward achieving financial independence, one diversified step at a time.

About the Author

T. S. AVINI is a writer who believes in the power of sharing life's lessons. Having faced hardship and pain, he turned to writing as a form of self-expression and healing. Today, he pours his heart into every book, aiming to help others navigate their own struggles and find strength in vulnerability.